YOUR BODY A BULLET

Elizabeth Vignali

&

Kami Westhoff

Published by Unsolicited Press
www.unsolicitedpress.com
Unsolicited Press books are distributed to the trade by Ingram.
Attention schools and businesses: Discount copies are available
for bulk orders. Please contact our team at
info@unsolicitedpress.com.

ISBN: 978-1-947021-69-3

YOUR BODY A BULLET

Elizabeth Vignali

&

Kami Westhoff

For Scarlet and Evelyn

For Naomia and Giorgi

TABLE OF CONTENTS

What's Left

(reed warbler mother to the cuckoo chick)

The common cuckoo practices brood parasitism: she lays her
egg in the nest of a different species than her own. Often, she
will time the laying so her egg will hatch first and her chick,
instinctively, will push the host mother's eggs from the nest.

The hollows of what would have been
my children pock the mud in mucky swallows—
not even the clamor of shattered shell
or broken bones, just the gulping absences
sunk among reeds and sweet-grass.

You are what's left to me.
You overflow the nest with your bawdy
striped breast and brash-budding hawk beauty.
I bring you leopard moths and rove beetles. I sing
you my drab brown song.

You gape your mouth
bigger than my head
and demand more.

I didn't know it would be so hard
to love you. I strive for connection while you sleep,
try to imagine you grown, wonder if I have
the same miscreant black feathers
hidden beneath my chest.

What kind of mother am I, doling out meals
with resentment lodged in my throat?
What miserly hand carved out my stature,
my flea-sized heart?

When I search for anything resembling
affection, all I see is my own tiny eye
engulfed like a stone
in the wide pool of yours.

Weighted Flight

(common cuckoo mother to her cuckoo chick)

You're mine, though your beak never split into mouth
at the sight of my weighted flight. Your bones, now bent
perpendicular in her twiggy nest, stretched free
in my yolky ovum. I taught you to thrust her eggs
from the nest the moment you hatched, blind and bare--
your first act of life. Her foreign song barks fluent
from your throat until her beak dips deep and you are fed
like you are many.

Your new mother is patient with you. Doesn't neglect
you as you grow three times her size, your feathers
a storm on the cusp of her nest. Perhaps doubt settles
in her chest like a cough, but she feeds you far longer
than she would her own, nearly killed by the task
of your appetite.

I'll never know why I don't build my own nest,
pinch the mealy bodies of beetles and caterpillars
and feed you myself. Or why I'm driven to stalk her,
sync our cycles like sisters so the moment she lay,
you spilled from my body like a twin.

You will leave her soon, her song forever imprinted
In your syrinx, to craft your own catastrophe.
She'll busy herself with the burden of your return,
wonder how next time she can make you stay.
She'll never admit it, but you are her favorite.
The ones we see least of ourselves in always are.

Once, I Served Only Myself

(*Leucauge argyra* spider to the *Hymenoepimecis argyraphaga* wasp)

The wasp paralyzes the spider and lays her egg. When the larva hatches and becomes ready for pupation, it injects a behavior-altering chemical into the spider that forces it to spin a web suited for the young wasp's cocoon. After spinning this strange web, the spider waits in the middle, motionless, to die.

You know me only as a host
but so does everyone—
no one has bothered to give me
a common name, a purpose
other than spinning
a strange web among purplehearts
and the limp leggy flowers
of the poponjoche.

Your young embellish
my stripes with spots,
infuse me with an elixir
that amputates my will.

They feed on me while I turn
your latent image visible—
string its sterling architecture
from branch to branch. The rain
washes it into existence.

Most animals aren't lucky
enough to know why
they're compelled to do
what they do. I have no questions
about God, just the irrefutable alchemy
of your infant apothecaries.

You're gone long before your design
appears between my legs
as if sketched by your hand, ghost
lines drawn and erased and drawn
again in wasp serum.

Once, I served only myself.

Depend Upon the Stilling

(*Hymenoepimecis argyraphaga* wasp to the *Leucauge argyra*
spider)

Think of it as a compliment. I searched millions
of years for the perfect web. I know
it is in your nature, but please don't resist, the prick
is worsened by wiggling. Be still. Breathe deeply.
The toxins spear through your body with each heartbeat.
Rest in the calm of paralysis.

My young cracks into life on your belly, latches
and feeds without question. Soon, as is the way
with the young, it decides the home you've built
won't do. It commands you to demolish
and rebuild, and its rudimentary instruction
unravels an unnamable inside you.

My young, still only mouth and throat and stomach,
approves the remodel, you tip toe to the web's simple center
and wait. The complex equations of weight, mass, resistance—
your birthright, no more yours than the constellations.
When it molts, its path to you is unpocked.
It will be over before you bother to care.
Your muscles frayed unrecognizable
from your brainless effort, relent.

If we could go back, what would we do differently?
Would I be given the gift of the web? You,
the formula of flight? Or would we merge:
winged, weaving, lay a thousand eggs
at the feet of our queen?

I'm long gone by the time you are drained and discarded,
but if I had been there, maybe I could've made it easier.
Enveloped you in the cape of my wings while you looked
out at stained-glass sky and imagined a world where the beat
of my young's heart didn't depend upon the stilling of yours.

The Assassins Have Marked Us

(*Sacculina*-infested crabs to one another)

Sacculina, *a type of barnacle, infests both male and female*
crabs and chemically castrates them. They then lay their own
eggs and force the crab to release hormones that cause it to
behave as though the Sacculina *eggs are its own. Humans have*
used Sacculina *to inhibit the spread of invasive crab species.*

The assassins have marked us with egg sacs, round
white dollops of cream. Our bodies a junkyard
on the ocean floor. Rusted old cars mottled red and orange.
Abandoned, and too numerous to count.

While we wait to labor, we amuse ourselves
by finding designs on each other's backs. Veined fleur di lis,
faces, trees. One sees a horse. One sees a devil.
One sees steam rising in yellow curls.

The males, too, wrapped in the urges of birth. No matter
our gender, we are all sisters now. If we were human,
we'd braid each other's hair, brew rosehip tea,
coach one another's labored breath.

Instead, when the unrelenting instinct takes us, we trample
each other to get out. The weakest are overturned. Claws
scrape over crenellated underbellies, batter brick shells, gouge
ditches in the sandstone that leads to the birthplace.

After, we nurture the aliens as if they were ours.
Swirl our claws in the sea, twist the saltwater into a dervish
to better flourish our extermination. We haven't lost
our own children, but you've ensured that it feels like we have.

We try to distract ourselves. Unfocus our eyes
and watch the patterns instead. One sees a galaxy,
one a black star. One sees a snowstorm.
One sees a dog at the door, scratching to be let out.

Surrogate

(*Sacculina* to the crab)

Don't worry. I promise you won't even know I'm there.
You won't claw at your shell as my tendrils ease
into your stomach and suck like a newborn. You'll scavenge
freely as I swallow your nervous system, stretch into the shell
of each leg, shroud your brain and make a mother out of you.

You carry my eggs as though they are your own,
forage with a renewed sense of purpose.
You feast on only the finest algae, snails, sea urchins,
Swear to friends you'd do anything to protect your own.
When it is time, I taste the water become saltier,
feel the gentle bob of your body encompassed
in the waves. Only when my eggs cloud the whirl
of ocean you created with your fussing do I wonder
which will inherit your wide-eyed stare,
which my tendency for over-attachment.

By the time they've scattered,
I will have poisoned your body sterile,
and you will wonder what you've done
to make the mates stay away. Blessed with the gift
of simplicity, you'll never know your young were mine.

You'll remember those weeks as the best of your life.
Back when everyone offered you theirs,
insisted upon the brilliance of your beauty,
clicked their claws against the swell of your belly,
as you blushed beneath your brick-red shell.

Pretty on the Inside

(female anglerfish to the male)

*The male anglerfish is much smaller than the female, and
doesn't develop sexual organs until he finds a female and
attaches himself to her. Attachment occurs when he nibbles
her skin and releases an enzyme that causes his lips to fuse
into her flesh until, ultimately, his body melts into hers.*

I can no longer discern where my body ends
and yours begins. You were the first who couldn't resist
my luminescent lure, the pheromones that saturated
your mind like a first-love centerfold.

For a time, I felt your fins' flutter, the pierce and tug
of teeth as my skin and muscle resisted then relented.
I queased as my vessels unraveled and rearranged
to make room for yours. You wear my body like a terrifying
          costume,
your mouth stuffed with teeth. Even my eyes, which once saw
what I looked at, saw what ours saw.

I get confused some days. Whose thoughts do I think?
Do I eat what you crave?
Do I fuck who you wish to fuck?
You still breathe with your own gills—
is there a just me at the bottom of a breath?

Today, I was found again. His teeth, though no less sharp, more a tickle than tear. His entry leaves me ravenous, so I eat something twice my size, don't give a fuck about the limits of the body. You throb, all gill and testicle, long ago absorbed into my warm slick, stable and certain, stubborn as an ancient and unknowable organ.

First Impression

(male anglerfish to the female)

In the ocean's depths I find you only
once I've lost my way.

Like the little fish tangled up in the dark.
Knotted in your grin.

Your lantern shines like a scene
from some deep-sea Christmas card,

a soft gleam that illuminates the white
plankton drifting in the cold dark.

I settle into your body like a child
sinks into snow. A child might sweep

their arms and legs, leave
the impression of an angel.

My impression is more pockmark
than snow angel. Just the hollow

of the body that touched you first,
before your belly buckled under the remains
of all the lovers who followed.

As If Light Could Ever Be the Answer

(amber snail to the green-banded broodsac)

*The green-banded broodsac is a behavior-altering flatworm
that causes the snail to seek the light it usually avoids. The
flatworm occupies the snail's eye stalk and pulsates, mimicking
the appearance of a caterpillar, so a nearby bird—the definitive
host—might be tricked into eating the parasite.*

You prod me, shrinking,
into the light. My tender
eye capitulates to your toothed
body, stretches to accommodate
the desire of your movement.

You hatched this craving
for light, the urge for the greenest
leaf, the highest branch. I trust
in all the wrong things: breeze
and bird, the bright scrutinizing
loupe of sun.

I glide up the pendulous sedge,
paint its stalk glossy, bend
it slender with my weight.

You pulse behind my sight,
your image inescapable,
soft-focus and all mouth.

One day soon a beak will split us,
slit you and my sight from its stalk.
The sun once again the nucleus of fear,
the grass stretched toward it
as if light could ever be the answer.

Something Came Along and Made Us Matter

(green-banded broodsac to the amber snail)

I know it seems unfair, but have you seen what I look like?
Teeth a flurry of cyclone, lips puckered like an asshole.
I blinked to life in a rancid puddle stuffed into skin the shade
of shit. Before you drank me in,

I drowned a thousand siblings.
Stamped my stump on their faces until their eyes burst
and I rose to your lips, slipped into your sweet pink mouth.

I take my time in the core of your body.
I am the adorable magnet pinning the precious first painting.
The plush lovey keeping the child in its own bed all night long.
Soon I erupt into the stalk of your eye, throb color into drab.
You are blinded, no longer afraid of sunlight,
and when it strikes we quiver and strobe
and I make you irresistible.

In another incarnation, we pinched each other's cheeks,
crushed berries and rubbed their blood onto our lips.
We tightened corsets until our ribs were more cave
than cage. Practiced first kisses on the backs of hands
we'd lotioned into silk. We promised we'd never forget
what we meant before something came along and made us
matter.

Offering

(*Cephalotes atratus* ant to the *Myrmeconema neotropicum* worm)

Myrmeconema neotropicum *is a nematode that infests South American gliding ants. Once infected, the ant's small black gaster expands and reddens until it looks like a ripe berry. The ant alters its behavior, foraging further than uninfected ants and elevating its berry-like gaster so a bird is more likely to spot the ant and eat it, continuing the life cycle of the parasite.*

You slipped like a breath into my body,
shocked my black bright. Though I'd dreamed
of such singular acknowledgement, I let you beg
for my blessing, and as your blip of a body
sank into mine, I absorbed your compliments
about work ethic, adaptability, my unparalleled
strength like a memory I never got to make.

We glided through the thick wet, the air like an ocean,
my legs flared like the freaky wings of a never-been.
I watched my family march into jaws and beaks,
the scent of warning deep in my gut like a famine.

Soon, you moved into my spacious globe
the thin tunnel of your body couldn't offer.
As you thickened with eggs, leaves pressed veiny
prints on the soles of my feet, and you lounged,
sway-backed and swollen, cozy in my core.

When it was time, you bulbed my gaster
with your thousands, sent it bobbing in a fit of crimson.

They'll say you made me do it. Lament the loss
of a such a strong worker, claim my contribution
as significant as any. But as I sauntered like a drunk
to the edge of the world, rested my jaw on a leaf,
shoved my ass skyward, I watched myself from the inky orbit,
a miniscule point of light and color,
a solitary offering to the unforgiving expanse.

Possession

(*Myrmeconema neotropicum* worm to the *Cephalotes atratus* ant)

They ask what's the point of a life cycle
bookended by shit, all for a vacation inside
your black and shiny body.

But hasn't everyone wanted to be
someone else for a while? Smudged
the line between enchanted and enchained?

Instead, ask what I wouldn't give
to trade my unremarkable white smoothness
for your coppery strength,

your thorned and devilish charm,
and the ability to fly—just briefly—
grasped in the safety of someone else's body.

I really am sorry my presence
curdles your defenses, thins your durable
armor to this useless liniment layer,

a barely-there barrier
between me and the fantasy
of what it's like to be you.

If there were another way, I'd take it.
I'd leave you tough and uneaten.
I'd leave you flying.

A Corner to Haunt

(shortfin mako shark to the snubnosed eel)

*The snubnosed eel, typically a scavenger, is also an
opportunistic parasite that has been found stretched along the
backbones of various fish species and even curled within the
heart of a shortfin mako shark. The eel simply chews its way
into the body of the host and lives within it, feeding on its
blood until the host eventually dies.*

Your rootless wandering led you to me,
your bloody and burrowing pansophy.
When I think about the ocean's vastness,
the practice is tenable, if your style
a bit extravagant. Your elbowing
graceless through my gills, your levered entrance
in the crook of my heart. Don't we all seek
a corner to haunt, some small space to fill?

Unfortunate eel. You caught one who was
already caught, and now you have nowhere
to go. Sharp body branched black in my red.
Your sheer opportunism did you in.
Mistaken plicate mouth devouring
a heart fated for someone else's feast.

Your Body A Bullet

(snubnosed eel to the shortfin mako shark)

Once I saw you--your body a bullet
through the brain of the ocean—nothing else
would do. I once pleasured myself gill-deep
in the bellies of shad, feasting until
the eggs threatened to burst through the slim straw
of my body. But times had gotten tough--
you found me feeding on the bitter milk
of a cod's spinal fluid. Your deep-space
eye saw me, a line of slick on its backbone,
and now I fatten in your heart's lumen,
lick blood from my fingers while you complain
you do all the work, that this wasn't what
you signed up for when you swam close, teeth bared
gills flared in a *What are you waiting for?*

Carving

(oak tree to mistletoe)

Mistletoe attaches itself to the branches of a host tree and punctures the bark with its haustoria—specialized roots which penetrate the host's cell walls and draw water and nutrients from it.

At first I was proud. Your leaves webbed
my branches green against the barren bright of fall.
You were worshipped, as virile as an erection,
hoisted on my shoulders like a hero.
I'd never felt so close to the sky.

The change was slow like the night's steal
of light from the days of December.
When I drank, your thirst quenched.
When I took a breath, light and air became the food
that throbbed the color into your leaves,
sharpened your barbs, bled bright into the berries
that promised, *Disaster.*

Trees aren't known for their ability to heed warning.
We stand still as rock against the whack of an ax.
We offer our skin to flame, ignite ourselves into ash.
We favor the strength of the root over the expanse
of the branch. We wait for something to change
us into something else.

At times like these, it's best to turn inward,
burrow through the rings of memory, settle
in the deep-dark fibers like a childhood tragedy.
Here, I've already died, but the message hasn't yet spread
to the surface. It sits heavy in the wood of the heart,
 its message simple as the carvings of first love initials.
The unsolvable equation of you plus me.

Spire

(mistletoe to the oak tree)

In your branches cathedrals gather,
twist in fine green tendrils. My clinging
runners curl ahead to scatter
in your bones. It feels holy,
doesn't it? Let me froth your marrow,
let me lather bells across your body,
let me in. Lovers should be close.

At first—a gleam, a rising spire
as your branches bare
white against the sky, your immaculate palms
lift to the sun. I'll scour your veins
clean, I'll lay my flat leaves on you,
I'll show you there's nothing to fear.

Release your leaves, dear.
Confide in the sky with salted breath,
invest devotion, pull gravity down
in little deaths. Let's watch them fall
together. Don't fret. I have enough
for both of us.

No Thought of the Surface

(grasshopper to *Paragordius tricuspidatus*)

*Paragordius tricuspidatus is a brain-manipulative worm that
infects grasshoppers and other insects through infested water
sources. The parasite grows until it fills the host's body and
then forces the grasshopper to jump into water so the worm
can exit the drowned insect and find another worm to mate
with.*

Your egg rolled like an eye on my tongue,
slid through the tunnel of my throat, cracked
in my bowels where you tangled yourself unsolvable.
To blame you would be to blame the bud for the burst
of its petals, the thirsty mouth for its swallow.

The pressure of your slippery edges worsens
as you complicate. You are closer to death than birth.
You mature, unravel, and make a suggestion.
Your wrath wing-snapped into language,
rubbed into warning along the skin of our flanks.

Soon I long for the rank of the pond,
yearn to split its skin with the splash of my body.
I think of my young. I think of legacy.
I think of the corn's sweet silk
as I press my feet into the pond's silt
with no thought of its surface.

Questions You Never Asked

(*Paragordius tricuspidatus* to the grasshopper)

Nothing but muscle and gut
to cut to the quick.
Find us after the downpour
by winecups and purple larkspur
in puddles thick with moss
and Gordian knots.

A ropy shimmer
as if the rain itself
has become ribbons
of slither and twist,
a tangle of reasons
to end.

Whisper our names
so you know why you do it.
Latinate prayers to the god of biology:
Paragordius tricuspidatus.
Parachordodes megareolatus.
Parachordodes lestici.

When you drown yourself
beside the false indigo,
we'll stream from your mouth
like tongues, like catechisms,
like unbreakable answers
to questions you never asked.

Once We Were Us

(red snapper fish to the tongue-eating louse)

Cymothoa exigua *is a parasitic crustacean that attaches itself to the tongue of a fish, sucking the blood until the tongue atrophies and falls off, at which point the parasite fixes its body to the existing tongue muscles and acts thereafter as a substitute tongue for the fish.*

It is true that I feared you before I knew you.
I'd heard of your slick-gilled entry, migration
to tongue once your body matured, the pain
that leaves one speechless. But you were as subtle
as oxygen when I breathed you in, and the clawed
clench that coaxed blood from my tongue
more suggestion than demand. And once it was gone,
your body rooted raw in my back of my throat, relief.

Imagine graphing the topography of tongue
from the fleshy arch of the pallet, craving texture
instead of taste, understanding the dimension of flesh,
muscle, and bone only by its resistance and surrender
to the tip of the teeth.

I know you will leave me soon. Maybe you'll slip
into the sea, rest among the sleek fins of eelgrass.
Or retreat into my stomach, where you'll disintegrate
into my last supper. It doesn't matter which.
Once we were us we could never be anything but.

I will swim along, tongueless, ignore the silver flick
of lives waiting to be ended, starve in slow motion,
until the sea surfaces me into a flash of pale
for the sky to swallow.

Stars I'll Never See

(tongue-eating louse to the red snapper)

Feel sorry for yourself, tongueless fish,
but know this: you are free as I am not.
You river through schools
of threadfin jack and sanddabs
and gesticulating fingers
of blue seagrass. You watch
the moon with your tarnished eye.

My life is spent within
your slick glistening. A poor
stand-in for muscle and taste,
the stunt double
for a dumb organ.
My mother always said
You can be whatever you want
when you grow up,
as long as it's a tongue.

A parasite must find wonders
in the small.
The syncopation of saltwater
and blood, the red-denned
oriental carpet mapped across
your mouthfloor. High above
my small head, your white bones
vault in cathedral arches,
Gothic arrows that point
toward stars I'll never see.

Labor

(bumblebee to the larva of the thick-headed fly)

The thick-headed fly injects the bumblebee with her egg, which hatches and manipulates the bee into burrowing into the soil. The larva will be safe to emerge there once it has eaten its way out of the host's body.

At first, you were just an itch. I shivered, leaned
into the spines of catmint, scratched with the dignity of a dog,
but I couldn't quite reach you. The queen, that bitch, ordered
me to keep working. I found a delphinium, wedged
into the folds of its mouth-pink petals, where your ache
spread like a pesticide—thirst choked my intestines, hunger
slit the split-second beat of my heart. I flew frantic, inarticulate
coordinates until I landed on a stone, sucked its nectar dry.

I longed for the shrike's skewer, the patient ambush
of a crab spider, or even the undignified underfoot squash
of a child. Without willing it, I dropped to the dirt at the base
of azalea, watched my legs dig deep into soil, the effort
more idea than action. I moved into the divot,
dirt dusted my body like pollen.

By then, you were more me than I, and would soon emerge
from the days-dead husk of my body. I thought of the queen,
perched on her extravagant pile of eggs. My co-workers
prepare for the hatching of an army of larvae. The thankless,
never-ending workday.
I imagined a deep breath of lavender and slipped into its calm.
Breathe in. Breathe out. Breathe in. Breathe out.

It is easier than one would think, accepting this final gift of the body.

Unfurl

(thick-headed fly to the bumblebee)

Let others spin it, try to make it pretty.
I have no soft words for you.
I will track your fidgety flight, follow
you while you fuss at the azaleas
like a nervous virgin. I won't insult you
with kinship despite our twin stripes,
the striking contrast of our black
and yellow. By the time you see me
I will already have carved you open,
stabbed my egg into your round belly.
I will not seduce you into believing
my young is yours. My child
will spider through your guts, sink deeply
into your need and siphon off
your own survival instincts.

There is no comfort even in death.
You've never seen the azaleas
from this angle before—the matte undersides
of the leaves, the pink blossoms
hidden from view. Even they have turned
their backs on you. My daughter will unfurl
from your body, emerge like a lover
from crumpled sheets, shake her wings
and lick her hands, the scent
of you still on her.

Everything You Could Have Been

(human to her parasitic twin)

*A parasitic twin results when identical twins do not fully
separate and develop unequally. One twin—the autosite—
grows into a relatively independent human, while the parasitic
twin stops developing and remains attached to the autosite to
varying degrees.*

I've seen photos of the others:
the boy with his small brown brother
head-first in his torso
as if searching for the rest of himself,
the girl child with four arms
and four legs like some ancient Hindu deity,
the man with legs spilling from his stomach.

I wear your face on my side.
Your eyes half closed so you don't look
upon the one who—if circumstances
were different—would have been a true reflection,
not this carnival mirror who magnifies
everything you could have been.

I wonder, again, how aware you are.
If you have a soul in there, or half a soul.
If you resent me for turning you into the part
human you are. An involuntary fetal magician:
Watch as I make my twin sister disappear!
Marvel at the incredible shrinking human!

Funny they call you the parasite
when I'm the one who took your life.
I brush your hair as if that could atone
for it. I wash your face, so much like my own.
With the sharp edge of my fingernail,
I sweep the yellow sleep from your eyes.

As Though We Were Meant to Be

(parasitic twin to her sister)

If it were up to me, I wouldn't change a thing.
I'm warm in the cave of your body, watching
you suffer in a world where we can't even be
imagined, your face a fleshy sliver through
my half-drawn eyes.

We can't blame their horror. What a sight--my head
sprouting from your side, hair slick and dark,
gnarled teeth desperate for the bite. Fifty years ago,
our mother could've sold us off as the headliner.
I'd let you do the talking, your answers quick
and final as gunfire, blink my reply, blush from the applause.
Instead, we're treated as though we were meant to be.
You have it far worse—my phantom limbs, desperate
for a torso, hook their toes under your ribs, out of reach
of the cough's release.

But, you are a good sister.
You pinch my hair near the root so the brush
doesn't tug. In the trough of cold season, snot runs
and you wipe it dry. Twice a day you say open wide
and brush my teeth, sing your ABCs to do it right.

Lately, there's been talk of surgery.
Promises of high success.
We both know our mother favors me,
whispers it so in my seashell ear when you drift off.

Our mother has suffered so much.
We will remember you in black and white,
all arms and legs, your edges smudged
like a redrawn. How easy it will be to life
just me, free from the burden of your limb-
ridden body, the real-life bust of the lost one.

.

About the Authors

Elizabeth Vignali is an optician and writer in the Pacific Northwest, where she coproduces the Bellingham Kitchen Sessions reading series. She is the author of *Object Permanence* (Finishing Line Press, 2014). Her poems have appeared in *Willow Springs, Cincinnati Review, Mid-American Review, Tinderbox, The Literary Review*, and others.

Kami Westhoff's work has appeared or is forthcoming in various journals including *Meridian, Carve, Third Coast, The Pinch, Decomp, Eclectica, Waxwing, Passages North, Redivider*, and *West Branch*. Her chapbook, *Sleepwalker*, won the 2016 Dare to Be Chapbook Contest from Minerva Rising Press. She teaches Creative Writing at Western Washington University in Bellingham, WA.

About the Press

Unsolicited Press was founded in 2012 and is based in Portland, Oregon. The team strives to produce exemplary fiction, poetry, and creative nonfiction. Learn more at unsolicitedpress.com.

CPSIA information can be obtained
at www.ICGtesting.com
Printed in the USA
BVHW072047161118
533335BV00002B/158/P